OMNIBOOTH

OMNIBOOTH

THE BEST OF

George Booth

CONGDON & WEED, INC.

NEW YORK

Other books by George Booth:

Think Good Thoughts About A Pussycat
Rehearsal's Off
Pussycats Need Love Too

Copyright©1984 by George Booth

Library of Congress Catalog Card Number: 84-70934

ISBN 0-86553-130-7
ISBN 0-312-92613-8 (St. Martin's Press)

Of the 226 drawings in this book, 213 appeared
originally in *The New Yorker* and were copyrighted©
in 1970, 1971, 1972, 1973, 1974, 1975, 1976, 1977,
1978, 1979, 1980, 1981, 1982, and 1983
by The New Yorker Magazine, Inc.

Edited and designed by Kenneth R. Hine

Published by Congdon & Weed, Inc.
298 Fifth Avenue, New York, N.Y.10001
Distributed by St. Martin's Press
175 Fifth Avenue, New York, N.Y.10010
Published simultaneously in Canada by Methuen Publications
2330 Midland Avenue, Agincourt, Ontario MIS 1P7

for Irene.

BOOTH

"The bagels are stuck to the ice cubes."

BOOTH.

*"If you ask me, this thing is going to get a whole lot worse
before it gets better."*

"*The United States Congress is urging all of us to produce more.*"

KEEPING WARM

Heated
BB boots.
← cork
Sew canvas boots.
Slip on over shoes.

Fill with hot BBs.
BBs heat fast in an iron skillet.

On sunny cold days, carry clothes in suitcase and quickly pinch on Kitchen-foil suit.

Turkey pan (foil $1.29) will work best for quick Pinch-on cap.

Heated tire irons wrapped in towels can be carried under one's topcoat.

BUS

Hot-water tie.
Warm all day at the office.

Face catnip comforter.

Variation of old N.Y. favorite — Hot-water pants.

Plastic is preferable.

These pants will help keep other folks warm on the bus.

← CORK

Trained-cat hat.

Chicken-wire underwear suit, with flashlight batteries in cap.

Leggings.

Handy snap-on hooks can be shaped from stovepipe wire.

Split, splice, and smoke long green-wood bow. Then lace two large pieces of cowhide with leather thongs to form Artificial opossum pouch.

Fill with opossums (8-12 as required). Stay warm all day. Not recommended for evening wear.

Chicken shoes. Very warm.

1.

2.

3.

And there is the old reliable Quart of whiskey.

BOOTH.

"Now, see here!"

BOOTH.

"I feel aggressive today. Not sexy — just aggressive."

"I have a stuffed chair and a rag rug that are going out in the spring sunshine today, Elsie!"

BOOTH.

"Oh-oh! There go Papa's timed-release vitamins!"

"He's nuts. She's nuts. All three young ones are nuts. The dog
is nuts. And the old lady upstairs is nuts, too."

"Was it a 'ittle putty tat?
'es it was. It was a putty!
Tum tum tum!
Tum on, pwetty putty,
tum det on Mommy's wap."

"You got here just in time, Mr. Lundquist. The boys are ready to give your transmission the gang gong."

*"From this day forward, we will do our very best to do unto
Pussy as we would have Pussy do unto us."*

"*I'm going to go have my hair done! I wouldn't go across the Sahara on a camel looking like this!*"

BOOTH

"When I get home tonight, remind me to call Babcock about the furnace."

"If Iggie Goldfarb wants to play 'Death of a Salesman' every morning of the year for thirty years, I say <u>let</u> Iggie Goldfarb play 'Death of a Salesman' every morning of the year for thirty years."

"Gram isn't one to say 'I told you so.' But if you recollect your wedding day some thirty-odd years ago, Gram did say you weren't getting the biggest slice of pie in town."

KEEPING FIT

Run through the parking lot once a day
and touch every car.

Imagine you have infiltrated
enemy territory and proceed
to your office under
hostile fire.

Climb stairs pretending
that only every fourth step
is safe.

BOOTH.

Hop to work on one foot. Hop home on the other.

Spend fifteen minutes each morning with a goat.

Dance along with Fred Astaire and Ginger Rogers.

Cycle to the county seat and climb the courthouse.

Take turns with your wife carrying one another around the house.

"Sire, we have peace."

"Give me a W. Give me an O. Give me an R. Give me a K. I want an E. I want a T. Give me an H and an I and a C."

"Let's not squabble with one another, Wes. As loyal conservatives, let us not squabble within the ranks."

BOOTH.

"What the hell do you mean you don't sell tickets to Larchmont?"

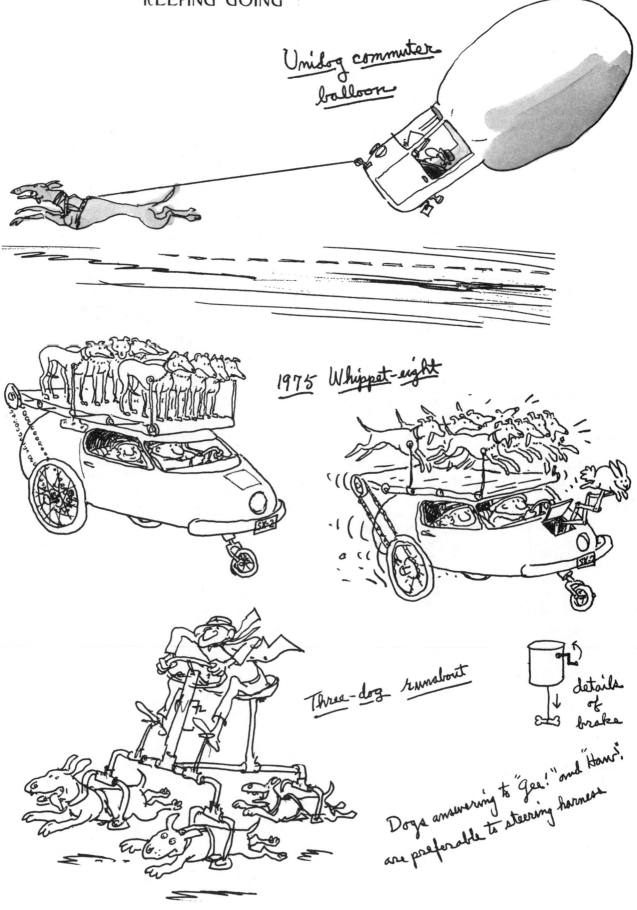

Unidog commuter balloon

1975 Whippet-eight

Three-dog runabout

details of brake

Dogs answering to "Gee!" and "Haw!" are preferable to steering harness

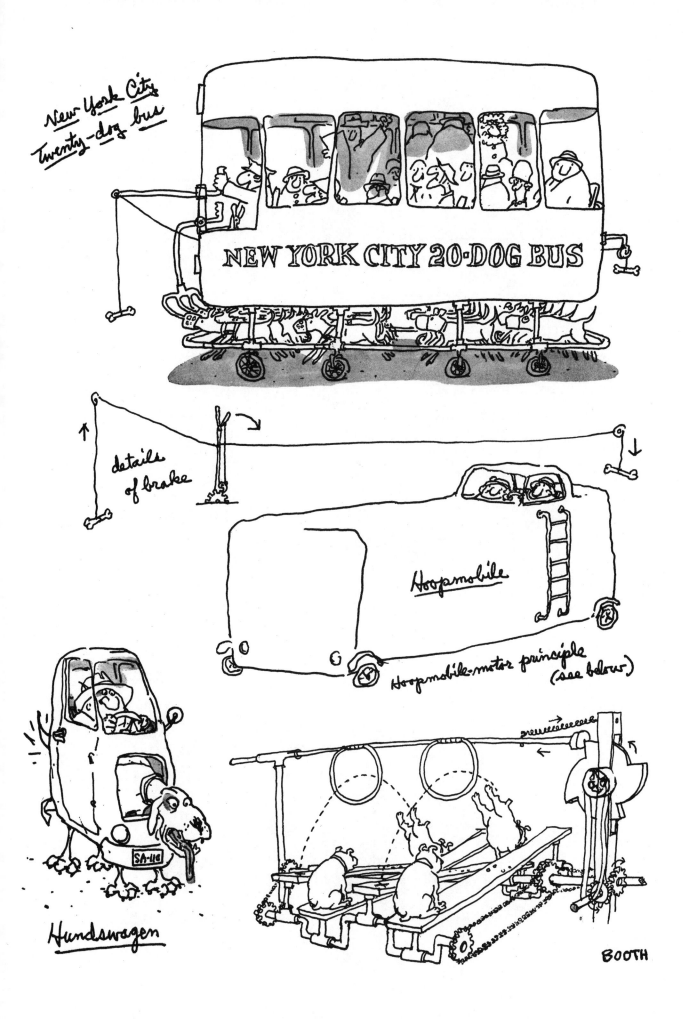

*"I'm in a bit of a rush this morning.
May I have just the shoeshine?"*

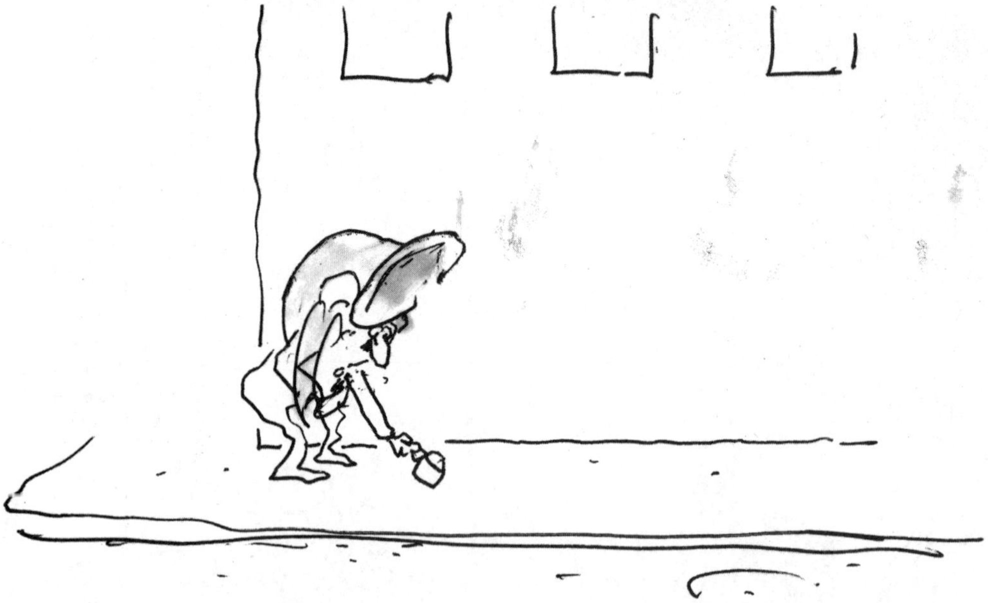

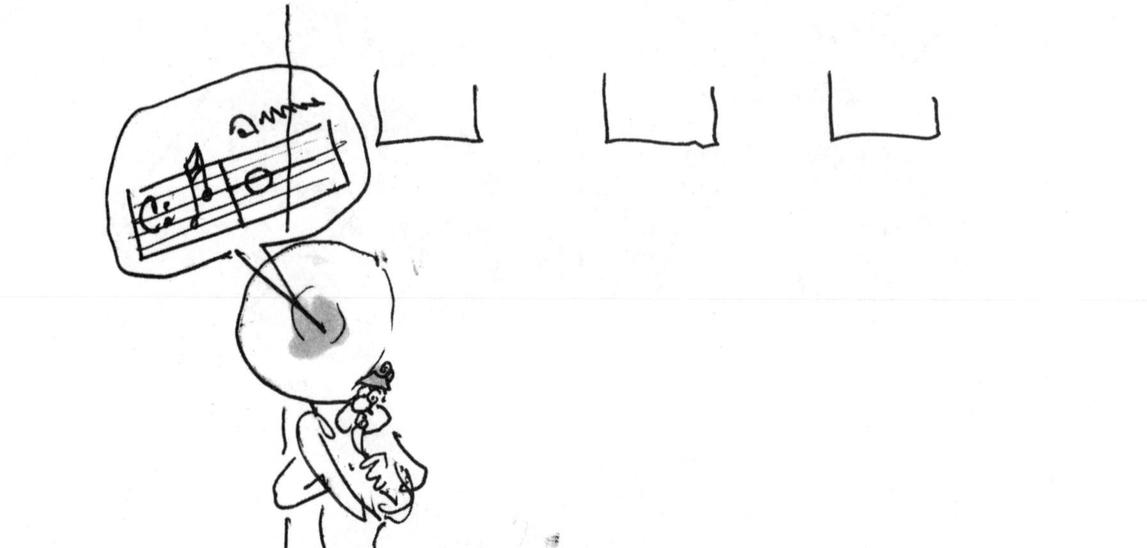

"Yeeaah!" "Yeeaah!" "Yeeaah!" "Yeeaah!" "Yeeaah!"

"Yeeeeeaaaaah!"

"Beulah has had four husbands, nine children, and twenty-three grandchildren, and God knows how many doughnuts she's served."

"If you can't get Riley to talk to you, Mr. Henderson, don't worry about it. He'll still fix your fuel pump. Riley, fix Mr. Henderson's fuel pump."

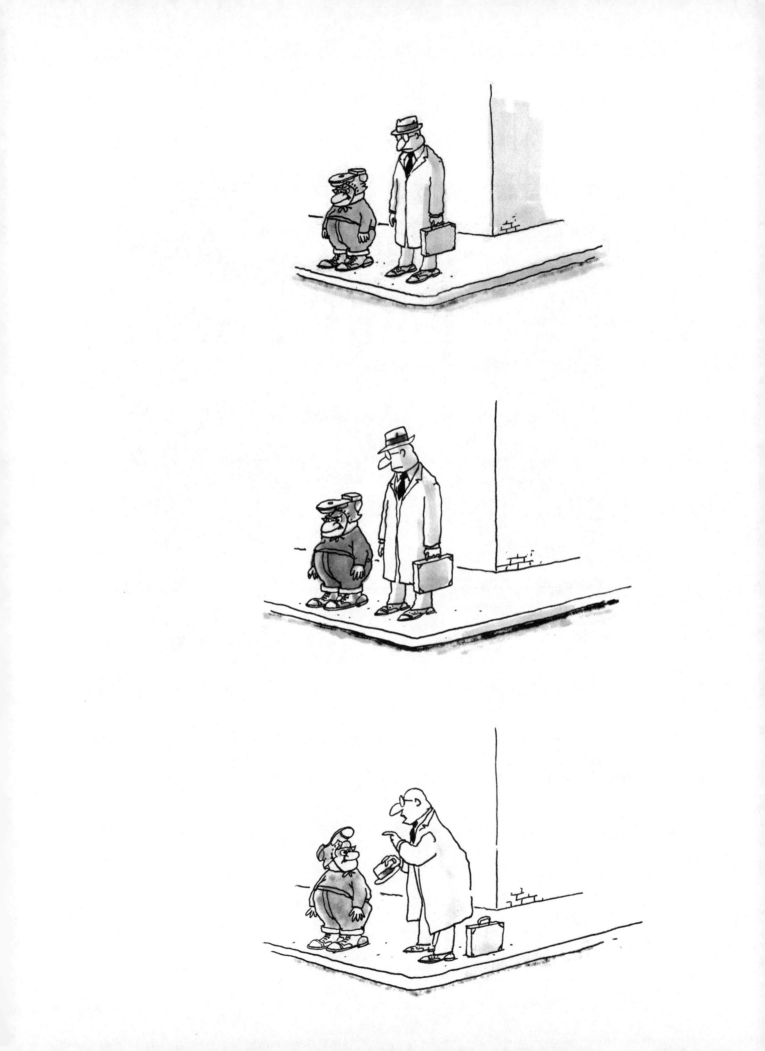

BOOTH

*"My fellow-employees, it is my painful duty to tell you
that discovery of a cash shortage was made this morning amounting
to some eighteen million dollars."*

"The men feel there is an evil spirit in your clutch housing. We've called a priest."

"Research and development."

BOOTH

"Not dogs today, Coontz! Today is piano music!"

*"You are not entitled to the Cuisinart food processor in this category, Miss
Dunwoodie. You are entitled to the Patty Cake stuffed monkey."*

STILL
OTHER
INVESTMENTS

Buttons. A group can get together and have one person do the buying.

Fruits and nuts can be dried at home in your spare time.

Peat.

Dirt-pushing machines.
Americans need to push dirt.

Bedsprings. Double your worth.

BOOTH.

If all else fails, improve
your relationship with your in-laws.

"Management has asked us all to tighten our belts a bit."

"We in the Postal Service move a hundred and six billion pieces of mail every year, and the volume is increasing. Ernie, what we are asking is: Could you move your pieces of mail a little faster than you've been moving them in the past?"

*"The Administration sees a quick recovery, but Mrs. Fisher
and I feel it's going to be deep and prolonged."*

BOOTH

"Having concluded, Your Highness, an exhaustive study of this nation's political, social, and economic history, and after examining, Sire, the unfortunate events leading to the present deplorable state of the realm, the consensus of the Council is that Your Majesty's only course, for the public good, must be to take the next step."

*"I'm going to give away all the cats and cancel my magazine subscriptions,
and then I'm going to paint ten pickets a day!"*

"... *the maid was in the garden hanging out the clothes,
along came a blackbird and snipped off her nose!*"

BOOTH.

"Jumpy and Jitter won't bother you unless you are selling something you ought <u>not</u> to be selling. What are you selling?"

"You get no interest on your account, Mrs. Dunwoodie, because your day of deposit and your day of withdrawal were the same damn day."

"If you withdraw or deposit your damn five dollars one more time this year, Mrs. Babcock, I'm going to shoot you!"

"She's going to run you a bit of money this time. Your entire ignition system has undergone what our chief mechanic, Mr. Murchison, terms a 'core meltdown.'"

BOOTH

"You give me my 'Cosmopolitan' or I'll whop you!"

BOOTH

*"All the pieces in this room are for sale except the
chifforobe. The chifforobe is <u>not</u> for sale."*

"My mother always says that. She always says 'You have to be a little bit crazy to live in New York.' Mother is a little crazy, but she doesn't live in New York. She lives in Nishnabotna, Missouri."

"Kaboom!"

*"Miss Dunwoodie is here to say goodbye to just getting by
and to say hello to a loan."*

BOOTH.

"Say! The Purple Onion wants impersonators."

"Write about dogs!"

BOOTH

BOOTH.

BOOTH.

*"Demand is steadily shrinking. Output is down. America has
no time to dillydally! What this country needs now is a song! An
open-your-wallets-and-spend-a-little song! An open-your-wallets-and-
spend-a-little song from the Hertzog Brothers!"*

*"Ferguson claims he's being whipsawed by inflation and taxes.
Whoops! There he goes now!"*

BOOTH

BOOTH

"Claypoole has his up days and he has his down days.
Today, he seems to be tipping over."

"Monthly charges for on-premises wire have been changed and the former wire charge has been separated into two components — a wire maintenance charge and a wire investment charge. If a central office access line charge appears on your detail of other charges and credits, it temporarily includes the wire investment charge. After completion of changes to our billing system, the wire investment charge will be a separate entry."

"Have you and your bear ever had a loan with us before?"

"Other folks have to pay taxes, too, Mr. Herndon, so would you please spare us the dramatics!"

"The average American drinker consumes twenty-four gallons
of beer per year, Foley, but not all in one night!"

"May I recommend our Spanakopita Special? It comes with your choice of drink and dessert, plus the Athenian Combo."

*"Broadbent is greater than a right angle but less
than a hundred and eighty degrees."*

"Your car will be ready, Mrs. Whittington, right after lunch."

"Aside from your three-dollar lottery ticket,
have you any collateral, Mr. Shelton?"

"The food is nothing special, but you do get quick service."

BOOTH.

"You can <u>not</u> 'miss July,' Miss Dunwoodie, because your loan is a pay-every-month loan, not a miss-a-month loan."

*"Broadbent has donated a philodendron to the club every year
for twenty-eight years. Broadbent is a good old boy."*

"Julia Child was cooking coq au vin and tambour parmentier this evening, and during her pommes en belle vue I burned your filet."

"I want it clearly understood that I am casting no aspersions on my wife's cooking. Heh heh, heh heh, heh heh, heh heh, heh heh heh, heh heh, heh heh, heh heh, heh heh heh, heh heh, heh heh, heh heh heh, heh heh . . ."

"Old Jesse located your trouble, Mr. Watkins, but he won't tell us what it is until after the ice-cream truck comes."

"That niche used to be the cigarette-machine niche, then it was the water-cooler niche, and now it's Mr. Pendleton's niche."

"Would you see to old Peterson? He's in the philodendron again."

"Harold ate my geranium."

*"Correction: The obituary for 'Ta Ta' Bottorff appearing in the November 12th
edition of the Post-News and Gazette-Telegram incorrectly listed 'Ebbie' Bottorff, of Spickert,
as the son of 'Ta Ta' Bottorff. 'Ebbie' Bottorff is the brother of 'Ta Ta' Bottorff, and also
we are pleased to say that <u>both</u> 'Ta Ta' Bottorff and 'Ebbie' Bottorff are living
and in good health. The Post-News and Gazette-Telegram regrets the error."*

"Teacher burnout."

"That metallic grinding means her throwout bearings are shot. She's backfiring through her carburetor. The tick indicates transmission trouble, and the smoke means she's on fire."

"We do understand what you are telling us, Miss Dunwoodie. You are taking your money out of our 'basket' and putting it in their 'basket' because in your opinion their 'apples' are 'better apples' than our 'apples.'"

"You dawdle, daydream. You make lists of things to do but can't get started. You seem to be restricted from doing what you know you should be doing. These problems will dissolve when you read Chapter Ten of my new book, at eight dollars and ninety-five cents."

BOOTH

BOOTH

"Hippety-hop, hippety-hop, hippety-hop."

"Hey, guys, you know what?"

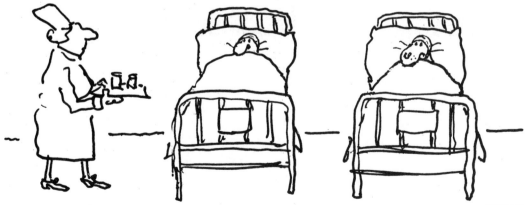

"It seems some days like I make a little progress, then other days it seems like I'm not getting anywhere at all."

BOOTH

"We may as well go home. It's obvious that this meeting isn't going to settle anything."

"She's all set, Mr. Ferguson, but don't go yet. We've got to get Rizzo
loose. His coveralls are snagged on her tailpipe bracket."

*"The pivotal issue, then, is not whether you respond to my
needs by cash or by check but for how much."*

"I see a vague figure of someone groping . . . groping . . . groping . . .
<u>*Yes, yes,*</u> *it's coming in more clearly now! It seems to be — yes, it is a man!*
The man has a briefcase! And some papers! The man is an economist!"

BOOTH.

"Your car will be right down, Mr. Lundquist."

"Murchison's theory is that it's dog hair in your fuel line."

"Bleeeeeeee-zoop! . . . Scratch . . . Attenshumb, blzk!"

"Threplek neck rack four . . ."

BOOTH.

"Thank you."

"I bought us an antique hat rack for when we have guests. It holds eight hats."

"We'll have to keep your car another day. There's a devilled egg in the carburetor."

"Attention, everyone! Here comes Poppa, and we're going to drive dull care away!
It's quips and cranks and wanton wiles, nods and becks and wreathed smiles."

"*Will your mother be coming down for dinner tonight?*"

"How about supper in the tub tonight, Hon?"

"If I were a surgeon, Mr. Ferguson, which I ain't, and your car was my
patient, which it ain't — except that it is, in a funny sort of way; that is, if you want
to look at it like that; you know what I mean — and you was her husband,
I'd have to say, 'Sir, your wife is going to need a valve job.'"

"This is the Main Street Bookshop. The copy of 'Nature's Way to a Two Week Face Lift' you ordered has come in."

"Mr. Swinehart has just crossed Route 36 at Goshen Junction. We are all expected, in exactly eighteen minutes, to greet him as he comes down the driveway."

"If you are fifty-five or older, you are liable at any moment to come completely unglued. Please call us, at the Glue Mutual Insurance Company. That's Glue. G-L-U-E. The Glue Mutual Insurance Company, at 800-176-5388. Now!"

"I'd just like to know what in hell is happening, that's all! I'd like to know what in hell is happening! Do you know what in hell is happening?"

"Leader Maloop, the people yearn for real answers."

*"And that's the opinion of Herman Fletcher. This
is Herman Fletcher, signing off."*

"Yee yee hee hee haw haw yip yip!"

"Yee yee hee hee haw haw yip yip!"

"She's just like her mother!"

"I call this spot Templeton's End, because this is where I dumped Old Templeton into the bog — Newport wheelchair and all."

"Oh, Lester! Not my macramé!"

Avoid overstimulation.

Reserve a few minutes each morning to recall the halcyon days of youth.

Spend more time alone.

Putter among the flowers before breakfast.

Take catnaps whenever you can.

Every now and then, drop a few dirty dishes in the disposal.

Stay single.

BOOTH

"You want __my__ opinion. __My__ opinion is that when push comes to shove, it will be more __bad news__ for the consumer."

"I think the Mayor's program is going to work."

*"Lots of folks say the Reagan program is going to make a clean sweep
of all our problems right away, but Mr. Pudney has stated that it will be
quite some time yet before we get things licked into shape."*

"This meeting was called in order to discuss the meat.
It has been pointed out that there is no more meat. A motion
has been made to fight over the bones."

"Chicken with forty cloves of garlic! How does that sound?"

"Edgar, please run down to the shopping center right away, and get some milk and cat food. Don't get canned tuna, or chicken, or liver, or any of those awful combinations. Shop around and get a surprise. The pussies like surprises."

*"There is no nourishment in this meal, but then, by the
same token, there is a minimum of poisons."*

"*Guess what, everybody. Mrs. Fancher is going to visit her daughter in Florida, and her Cissus rhombifolia is coming to stay with <u>us</u> for a few weeks.*"

"There goes Daddy to the park again! And do you know what he does in the park? He sits! That's what he does. He sits! He goes to the park and just sits!"

"Uncle Purvis was a man of high ideals. He subjected himself and his motivations to such rigid scrutiny that he rarely met his own standards. He never did anything."

"*The way I see it, Wendy, you only go around once.*"

"Aphids on the heliotrope!"

"Lately, everything has been getting on his nerves, Doctor. The credit people, the flooded basement, Mother's complaining about not getting enough zinc, Jimmy Carter. I just mentioned that our neighbor, Mrs. Uminiwitz, was going to split her big white peony, and it seemed to be more than he could take."

"I understand the house is a mess inside."

ORDER

Buying one-color socks
eliminates pairing.

Baskets of stuff stacked against the walls
conserve fuel, and get the stuff out from underfoot.

For small rooms, a table hoist is a must.

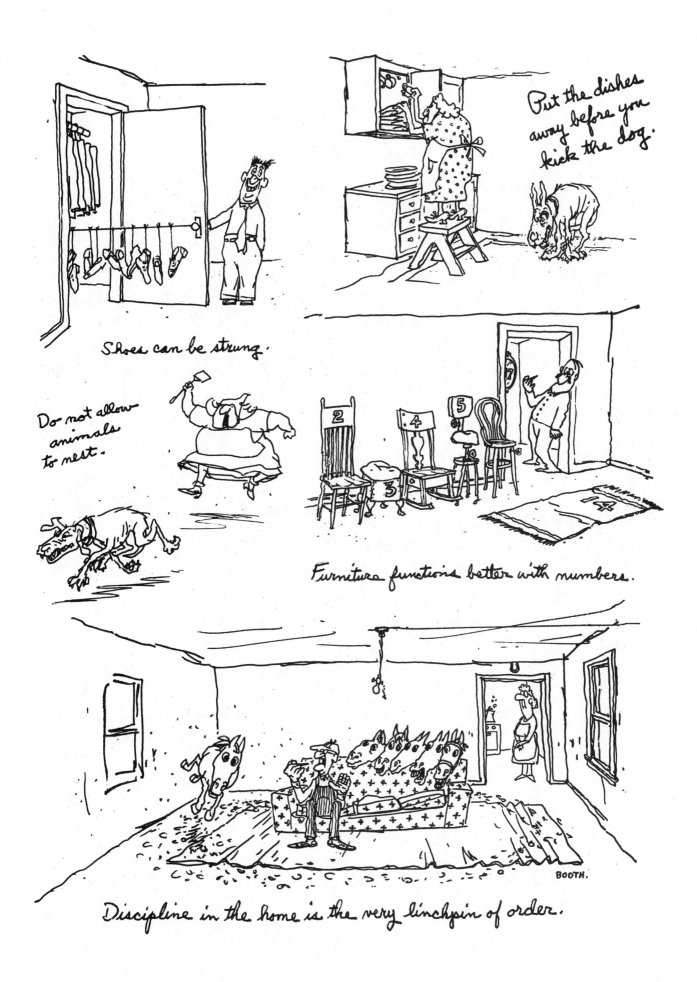

Put the dishes away before you kick the dog.

Shoes can be strung.

Do not allow animals to nest.

Furniture functions better with numbers.

Discipline in the home is the very linchpin of order.

BOOTH.

"How time flies! It was just thirty years ago tonight that you first ran me a hot bath — right here in this very tub."

"Oh, good! The bank says I have some money! That's good! Because I had a feeling I didn't have any money in there! Whoooeee!"

"*Before the break is over, I'm going to introduce you to our first violinist, Mrs. Ritterhouse. After one has had a good long talk with Mrs. Ritterhouse, all the barnacles let loose and fall off and one sits higher in the water. Here, have another watercress sandwich.*"

"We have certainly tamed the once wild beast of inflation."

*"We will intensify our attack on the morality of the country, step up our pornography
campaign, infiltrate the media, and further undermine political, educational, and religious institutions.
We'll stir up the old ethnic suspicions and spread rumors about shortages and rationing.
Then we'll top it all off with a whole new era of earsplitting psychedelic rock!"*

"Bavoom!"

"Rehearsal's off! Our first violinist was apprehended early this morning poaching clams in Great South Bay! The authorities have confiscated her rake and long tongs!"

*"Harry, I wish you'd stop singing 'The Impossible Dream' and
help me feed the pussies once in a while."*

"Roy, Jr., is all stems. He grew in the shade."

"One day at a time, Ethel, I take it one day at a time. So far this year,
it has been the usual assortment of useless junk. Last week, he located a dump scow,
and he spent all _this_ week dragging a 1929 Ford engine block out of the river.
Sunday, he made himself sick — thought he had a pirate's gewgaw,
but when the mud came off, it turned out to be an ice-cream-freezer crank.
I take it one day at a time, Ethel, one day at a time."

*"Say something nice to me, Luke. Not anything common. Something that
will rekindle smoldering passions, stoke the memory of half-forgotten follies,
and make the fountains of my spirit flow again."*

"How would I rate, hon, on a scale of one to ten?"

"Mrs. Leffler says lots of men settle for the first skirt that comes along and then spend the rest of their lives regretting it. Luther, was I your first skirt?"

"By Jupiter, an angel! Or, if not, an earthly paragon!"

"Do you know what I'm going to do? I'm going to pull my hat down over one eye and frizzle my hair."

"That's my son, Douglas, Mrs. Eichenholty. He has been in perpetual rebellion since the early sixties. Just step over him, please."

"Now hear this! Mr. Wetzel is prepared to comply with state and
federal emission-control standards if and when they become effective.
Until such time, Mr. Wetzel will continue to indulge himself in the
manner to which he has become accustomed. That is all."

"*We were minding our own business when the paddy wagon pulled up and took the good girls with the bad girls.*"

"Are they still fighting organized crime or have they decided to let it alone?"

"Now, last time, near the end of Ravel's 'Bolero,' I heard a scream."

"I'm just trying to figure out <u>when</u> I'm going to do <u>what</u> for Christmas."

"It's time to pay the fiddler."

"I feel in an upbeat mood."

"*From the top — 'Watermelon Man.' Let's sock it out and give Mrs. Ritterhouse a chance to really cook!*"

"Uncle Whit was country when country wasn't cool."

"There are few moments in music so thrilling as when Brucie and Mrs. Ritterhouse start riffing in tandem."

"Isabelle Isley wants to join the Ivy Society.
All she has is a Virginia creeper. Ha!"

"The Schoonover sisters' cotton batting is loose."

BOOTH

"Like a duck. Calm and placid on the surface, but paddling like hell. That's me!"

BOOTH

"*The bugs got your little drop-leaf table.*"

"The start of a new season is a welcome time for all of us. Winter gives way to spring, and pleasant childhood memories are revived. Play ball!"

"It's sixteen hundred dollars for August, including gas, electricity, maintenance, beach sticker, and old Mrs. Pennington up in the attic."

"Your bill comes to forty-eight dollars more than we estimated, because that little black thing with a lot of wires going into it needed fixing."

"I want you to start thinking about someone <u>new</u> at our house. I want you to start thinking good thoughts about a pussycat."

BOOTH

*"The Yard of the Month for August has been chosen by the Mount Purvis Garden Club.
The winner is Mrs. Ruth Easton-Smith. The club has also chosen your yard, Mr. Brindlehope, to receive
honorable mention. Both yards will be announced in the 'Mount Purvis Call.' "*

"Frank fretted for years about developing, as he put it, 'a pear shape,'
and I'd always say, 'Frank, honey, don't worry about it,' but I have been
thinking he's right to be concerned and I should be honest and say to him,
'Frank, honey, you have developed a pear shape, and you should do
something about it.' Don't you agree, Mrs. Rosenquist?
Yoo-hoo! Frank, honey..."

"Jesse, isn't that one of Mr. Ferguson's wheels?"

"That, honey, is probably an end."

"*While we were in Westchester — on a whim, mind you — Harold and I turned in to a drive-in movie and saw 'Honky Tonk Freeway.' It ruined our August.*"

"Mr. Pudney says Irma can soak that old chair he found, reshape it,
weave in some new wicker, replace the seat, paint it, and — bingo!
She'll have herself a hundred-and-fifty-dollar chair!"

*"A word to the wise, Lucille. Only mad dogs and Englishmen
go out in the midday sun. One lump or two?"*

"The Armentrout brothers never achieved much success in the business world, but they <u>have</u> caught <u>lots</u> of butterflies."

"Today has been difficult, Lucille. Wellington foozled his drive at the ninth tee, and the people next door adopted a new pale-fawn Siamese cat."

*"You never liked my baking-powder biscuits because they're not your
mother's baking-powder biscuits! You'll never like anybody's baking-powder
biscuits if they're not your mother's baking-powder biscuits!
You're pigheaded, Harold! Plain and simple. You're pigheaded!"*

"Once it catches on, the small-horse household-pet idea will go like blazes.
And you may quote Mr. Pudney on that."

"I __ask__ you. If not the Reagan Administration, who? If not now, when?"

"Lots of people complain about the weather, but Bul is the only one I know who <u>does</u> anything about it."

"*Rudyard is becoming incensed over the way congressmen can be bought.
When he gets mad enough, he'll cut the grass.*"

BOOTH.

"You should try race walking. It's better for you than running.
It's good for your cardiovascular system, and at the end of fifteen minutes
your glands excrete a juice that will make you happy."

"Nineteen cricket trills in fifteen seconds. Add forty. The temperature is approximately fifty-nine degrees Fahrenheit."

"Mrs. Ritterhouse had a dream last night. She dreamed about firm, fresh
cucumbers, their skins uncoated with shelf-life-extending goop; tender zucchini and sweet corn;
red, ripe, juicy tomatoes; big bunches of piquant basil; sprigs of herbs such as
tarragon and sage. It's the same dream she had last year in February."

"You filled an old tire with marigolds. I never said a word. You planted
petunias in a potbellied stove. I kept my mouth shut. You put geraniums in the birdbath.
I didn't say anything. This morning, you filled that damned old white enamel washing machine
with morning glories, and <u>now</u>, by God, I'm going to say something."

"I __do__ apologize, Rinehart. The cat has never bitten anyone previously."

"George Stoner is here from Terre Haute. He and Henry are talking over old times."

"I'm sorry to interrupt the più mosso, but Mrs. Patterson informs me the cat has passed away."

"Sunset and evening star,
And one clear call for me!
And may there be no mourning at the bar,
When I put out to sea . . ."

"This is your anchorman, John Moore, saying, 'That's all there is. There is no more.'
Until tomorrow at the same time, when there will be more."

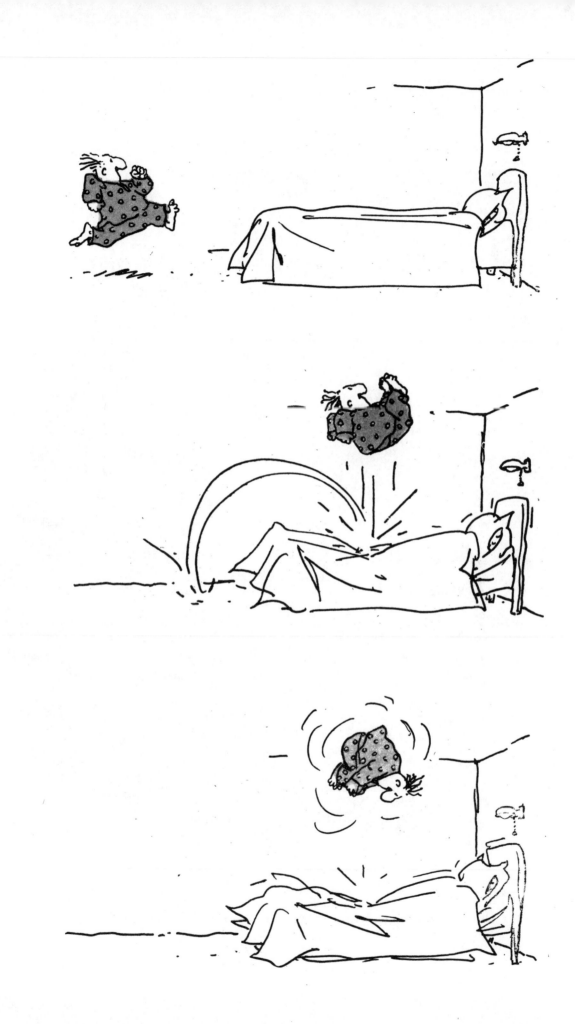

SECURITY

Geese will still do the job.
And you can always use the eggs.

Self-employed types tend to
roam their properties during
the night. This is good.

It is difficult these days to get
well-stocked moats out of one's mind.

Burglars hate the old
wire-coat-hanger alarm.

Those in the know wear a police
cap during afternoon-saunter time.

Scatter fake jewelry all over the place. (Make a
mental note of where you put the good stuff.)

Rig a trip wire to
set off Ravel's "Boléro."

Blow a whistle every now and then.
These are not ordinary times.

BOOTH

*"Ernie, Bernard, and Lou Ella Grosbeck are here with Professor
Hankins and some horticulture people. Professor Hankins and the horticulture
people have never seen a night-blooming jasmine."*

"We could stand a little easing of the crunch down here."

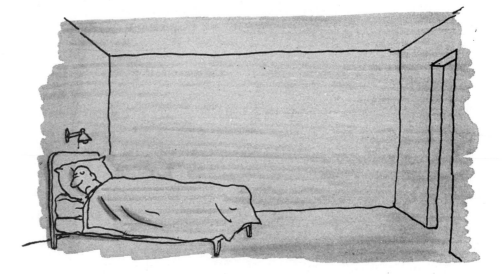

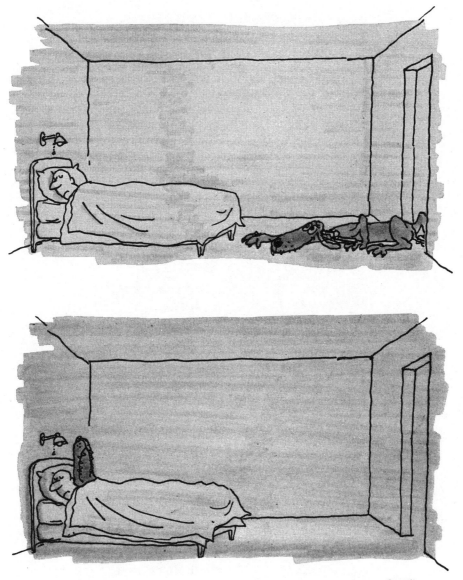

BOOTH.